The AI Billionaire: The new normal

By Megbo Beauty

Table of Contents

Introduction: AI Billionaire: The New Normal

The groundbreaking potential of artificial intelligence (AI) has captivated the world and transformed industries across the globe. From self-driving cars to virtual personal assistants, AI has revolutionized the way we live, work, and interact. In the book "AI Billionaire: The New Normal," we delve into the remarkable rise of AI and its profound impact on society.

Chapter 1: The Rise of AI

In this first chapter, we explore the origins and the rapid advancement of AI technology. We delve into the early beginnings of AI, tracing its roots back to the pioneering work of Alan Turing and other visionaries who laid the foundation for what would become one of the most transformative technologies in human history.

As we journey through history, we witness pivotal moments that propelled AI into the mainstream. From breakthroughs in machine learning algorithms to the development of neural networks and deep learning, we witness the exponential growth and refinement of AI capabilities.

We also shed light on the key players who have shaped the AI landscape. We explore the contributions of renowned researchers, entrepreneurs, and corporations who have invested in AI research and development. From academic institutions to tech giants, these trailblazers have played a crucial role in pushing the boundaries of AI innovation.

Furthermore, we delve into the various domains where AI has made a profound impact. We examine how AI has transformed industries such as healthcare, finance, manufacturing, and entertainment. We explore real-life examples of how AI has optimized processes, improved efficiency, and even revolutionized customer experiences.

However, with the rise of AI comes a myriad of challenges and concerns. Throughout this chapter, we address the ethical, legal, and societal implications of AI. We delve into the ethical dilemmas surrounding AI-driven decision-making, job displacement, and data privacy. We also discuss regulations and policies aimed at ensuring responsible AI development and use.

Finally, we explore the potential future of AI, examining emerging trends and possibilities. From the integration of AI with other cutting-edge technologies like blockchain and robotics to the potential for AGI (Artificial General Intelligence), we delve into the exciting and sometimes controversial future that awaits us.

Conclusion

As we conclude this introductory chapter, it becomes evident that AI is more than just a buzzword or a fleeting trend – it is the new normal. The rise of AI has not only transformed industries but also the very fabric of our society. In the pages that follow, we will delve deeper into the profound impact of AI on different sectors and explore the potential it holds for the future. "AI Billionaire: The New Normal" is a comprehensive guide that navigates the complex world of AI, providing insights and perspectives from experts in the field. Together, let us embark on this journey to understand and embrace the incredible possibilities that AI presents.

Chapter 2: The Secret Life of a Silicon Valley Billionaire

In this chapter, we delve into the secretive and often enigmatic world of Silicon Valley billionaires and their intricate relationship with AI. These tech titans have amassed unimaginable wealth and influence through their innovative ventures, many of which are deeply intertwined with AI technologies.

One prominent Silicon Valley billionaire who has become synonymous with AI is Elon Musk. As the CEO of Tesla, SpaceX, and Neuralink, Musk has been at the forefront of AI development and its potential impact on society. Musk's vision for the future centers around achieving an AI-driven world that benefits humanity rather than poses risks. He has consistently advocated for the responsible and ethical development of AI, warning about the dangers of AI surpassing human intelligence and potentially leading to undesirable outcomes.

Another notable figure in the tech industry is Jeff Bezos, the founder of Amazon. While not primarily associated with AI like Musk, Bezos has spearheaded the integration of AI into various aspects of Amazon's operations. From AI-powered recommendations and personalization algorithms to the use of robotics in Amazon's warehouses, the company has leveraged AI to revolutionize the e-commerce industry. Bezos's wealth and influence have allowed him to explore other AI-related ventures, such as Blue Origin, his space exploration company.

Furthermore, we cannot discuss Silicon Valley billionaires without mentioning Mark Zuckerberg, the CEO of Facebook. While Facebook is primarily a social media platform, AI plays a pivotal role in its functioning. AI algorithms power content recommendations, ad targeting, and even the detection of harmful content.

Zuckerberg's focus on AI extends beyond Facebook, as he has famously invested in AI research and development through initiatives like the Chan Zuckerberg Initiative.

These examples highlight the close ties between Silicon Valley billionaires and AI, as they actively seek to capitalize on the transformative potential of this technology. Their immense wealth and influence have propelled AI research, development, and implementation to unprecedented levels.

However, the actions of these billionaires have also sparked controversies and debates. The ethical implications of their endeavors, such as data privacy concerns and AI-driven decision-making, have raised questions about the concentration of power in the hands of a few individuals. The influence of these billionaires extends beyond technological advancements, shaping societal norms and perceptions of AI.

Moreover, the chapter also sheds light on the philanthropic efforts of Silicon Valley billionaires in the field of AI. We explore initiatives like OpenAI, co-founded by Elon Musk and others, which aims to ensure that AI benefits all of humanity. Through projects like this, billionaires are attempting to foster collaboration and responsible AI development, recognizing the need for shared knowledge and resources in the pursuit of AI's potential.

In conclusion, Chapter 2 delves into the intriguing world of Silicon Valley billionaires and their connection to AI. Through their ventures and initiatives, these billionaires have left an indelible mark on the AI landscape, reshaping industries and society as a whole. However, their influence also raises important questions about the concentration of power and the societal impact of their actions. Understanding the secret lives of Silicon Valley billionaires provides us with insights into the motivations, vision, and potential consequences of their AI-driven ventures.

Chapter 3: AI Takes Over the Stock Market

Introduction:

Artificial intelligence (AI) has made significant inroads in various industries, and one sector where its impact is particularly pronounced is the stock market. In this chapter, we explore how AI has revolutionized stock trading, providing unparalleled accuracy, speed, and efficiency. We delve into the different ways AI is utilized in stock market analysis and decision-making, highlighting examples of successful AI-driven trading strategies.

1. AI-Powered Trading Algorithms:

AI has paved the way for the development of sophisticated trading algorithms that can analyze vast amounts of data, make predictions, and execute trades swiftly. These algorithms, often referred to as "robo-advisors," have gained popularity among individual investors as well as financial institutions.

One prominent example is the hedge fund Renaissance Technologies, led by mathematician and former codebreaker James Simons. Renaissance Technologies relies heavily on AI and machine learning algorithms to analyze market data and generate high-frequency trading strategies. The fund has consistently outperformed traditional investment approaches, showcasing the power of AI in stock market trading.

2. Sentiment Analysis:

AI is also used to analyze social media sentiment, news articles, and public opinions to gauge market sentiment accurately. Machine learning algorithms can process vast amounts of text data, extracting valuable insights that traditional analysis may miss. By interpreting the collective sentiment, AI can predict market movements and identify potential opportunities or risks.

One notable example is the hedge fund Two Sigma, known for its AI-driven investment strategies. Two Sigma's AI models analyze textual data from various sources, including news articles and social media platforms, to derive sentiment trends. This analysis assists with the fund's decision-making and can lead to profitable trades.

3. Natural Language Processing and News Analysis:

AI algorithms equipped with natural language processing (NLP) capabilities can interpret news articles and company reports, extracting relevant information for trading decisions. NLP allows these algorithms to process and understand human language, enabling them to identify insights, sentiments, and trends that impact stock prices.

For instance, the company Kensho Technologies developed an AI-powered platform that can quickly analyze news articles and generate actionable trading insights. By combining NLP with machine learning algorithms, Kensho Technologies provides investors with real-time information on how specific news events may influence stock prices. This technology has been adopted by major financial institutions, including Goldman Sachs, to support their trading activities.

4. Pattern Recognition and Technical Analysis:

AI excels at recognizing patterns and identifying trends in large datasets. In stock trading, AI algorithms can detect subtle patterns in historical price and volume data, aiding in making predictions about future market movements. This approach, known as technical analysis, has been used for decades but has been significantly enhanced by AI capabilities.

For example, the company Kavout developed an AI platform capable of analyzing thousands of stocks simultaneously using technical indicators. The platform employs machine learning algorithms to identify patterns that indicate potential buying or selling opportunities. This AI-driven approach to technical analysis has attracted the attention of both individual and institutional investors seeking to improve their trading strategies.

Conclusion:

AI has transformed the stock market by providing advanced analytical capabilities, real-time information processing, and powerful decision-making tools. The examples explored in this chapter highlight the various ways AI is utilized in stock trading, from high-frequency trading to sentiment analysis and technical analysis. AI-driven trading strategies have proven to be successful, enabling investors to make more informed decisions and potentially earn higher returns.

However, it's important to note that AI-driven trading also raises concerns. The rapid pace at which AI can process data and execute trades may exacerbate market volatility, exacerbate market manipulation, and amplify risks. Regulatory frameworks and monitoring mechanisms need to be in place to ensure that AI is used responsibly in the stock market.

Overall, AI's increasing dominance in the stock market signifies a significant shift in the way trading is conducted. As algorithms become more sophisticated and datasets grow even larger, AI's role in the stock market will continue to expand, shaping the future of the industry.

Chapter 4: The Dark Side of AI

Introduction:

Artificial Intelligence (AI) has undoubtedly emerged as one of the most influential and transformative technologies of the modern era. Its potential for improving lives, driving economic growth, and solving complex problems is unparalleled. However, as AI systems continue to advance in their capabilities, we must also be aware of the dark side that lurks within this technology. In this chapter, we will explore the ethical, social, and economic implications of AI, shedding light on its potential dangers and discussing real-world examples that exemplify the darker aspects of AI.

1. Bias and Discrimination:

One of the biggest concerns surrounding AI is its susceptibility to biases and discrimination. Machine learning algorithms are trained on vast amounts of data, which may unknowingly contain societal biases. As a result, AI systems can perpetuate and amplify these biases, leading to discriminatory outcomes. A famous example of this is the case of Amazon's AI recruiting tool, which displayed a bias against female candidates due to its training data being predominantly male-oriented.

2. Privacy and Surveillance:

AI technologies involve the collection, analysis, and utilization of vast amounts of personal data. This raises significant privacy concerns as AI systems can infringe upon individuals' privacy rights. One notable example is the rise of facial recognition technology, which has the capability to track and identify individuals without their consent. In countries with limited regulations, this technology has been used for mass surveillance purposes, eroding privacy and civil liberties.

3. Automation and Job Displacement:

AI's automation capabilities have the potential to disrupt traditional employment models and lead to job displacement. As AI systems become more advanced, they can replace human workers in various sectors, leading to unemployment and economic inequality. The automation of tasks previously performed by humans also places a burden on workers to upskill themselves in order to remain relevant in the job market. For example, automated chatbots have replaced many customer service representatives, resulting in significant job losses in the industry.

4. Deepfakes and Misinformation:

AI technology has enabled the creation of deepfakes, which are highly realistic manipulated multimedia content that can be used to deceive and spread fake information. Deepfake videos, audio clips, and images can easily be created and distributed, making it challenging to discern the authenticity of media. This has serious implications for individuals, organizations, and national security, as deepfakes can be used for malicious purposes such as misinformation, blackmail, or political manipulation.

5. Autonomous Weapons and Ethical Dilemmas:

AI's application in the military and defense sectors has raised concerns about the development and deployment of autonomous weapons. The concept of weaponized AI, where lethal decisions are made by machines without human intervention, raises ethical and moral dilemmas. The lack of accountability and responsibility in autonomous weapon systems can lead to unintended consequences, escalating conflicts, and compromising human lives. Organizations like the Campaign to Stop Killer Robots have been actively raising awareness about the dangers associated with these technologies.

Conclusion:

While AI provides immense opportunities for progress and innovation, we must confront the dark side that accompanies its rapid development. Bias and discrimination, privacy concerns, job displacement, deepfakes, and autonomous weapons represent just a few of the ethical and societal challenges associated with AI. Governments, organizations, and individuals must work collectively to address these issues through robust regulations, transparency, and ethical frameworks that ensure AI is developed and implemented responsibly, ultimately minimizing its negative impact on society.

Chapter 5: AI vs. Humanity

Introduction:

As Artificial Intelligence (AI) continues to advance at an unprecedented pace, concerns about its impact on humanity have grown in both scale and intensity. The potential benefits of AI are immense, but the question remains: how do we ensure that AI serves humanity rather than replacing or overpowering it? In this chapter, we will delve into the complex relationship between AI and humanity, exploring the ethical, social, and philosophical implications and examining real-world examples that highlight the challenge of maintaining a harmonious balance.

1. Threat to Employment:

One of the prominent concerns surrounding AI is its potential to replace human workers in various industries. As AI systems become more sophisticated, they can perform tasks with greater speed and accuracy, leading to fears of widespread job displacement. For example, advances in automation have significantly reduced the need for manual labor, raising concerns about unemployment rates and the potential erosion of job security for millions of workers.

2. Humanoid Robots and Social Interaction:

The development of humanoid robots, designed to mimic human appearances and behaviors, raises fundamental questions about human identity and social interaction. As these robots become more lifelike, they blur the lines between machines and humans, challenging our understanding of what it means to be human. The emergence of empathetic AI companions, such as Pepper the robot, suggests a future where AI systems may replace human companionship, leading to potential isolation and affecting human well-being.

3. Ethical Dilemmas and Decision-Making:

AI systems, particularly those driven by machine learning algorithms, possess the ability to make autonomous decisions based on vast amounts of data. This raises ethical concerns as AI algorithms may lack the capacity for empathy and moral judgment. The infamous example of the "trolley problem" in autonomous vehicles highlights the challenging ethical dilemmas faced by AI: should a self-driving car prioritize the safety of its passenger or pedestrians in an unavoidable accident? These decisions pose a moral burden and necessitate careful consideration of ethical frameworks for developing AI systems.

4. Loss of Human Creativity:

While AI can surpass human capabilities in certain tasks like data processing and pattern recognition, it is yet to match human creativity and innovation. AI systems can analyze large datasets quickly, but they struggle to replicate the intuitive leaps, emotional intelligence, and imagination that humans possess. Concerns arise regarding the potential loss of human creativity and the impact it may have on fields such as literature, art, and scientific discoveries, where a unique human perspective is critical.

5. Dependency on AI and Loss of Skills:

As AI systems become more prevalent and capable, there is a risk of over-reliance and diminishing human skills. Technology amplifies human efficiency, but excessive dependence can lead to a decline in essential skills such as critical thinking, problem-solving, and decision-making. For instance, with the convenience of voice assistants, humans may lose the ability to retain information or think for themselves, potentially diminishing cognitive abilities and autonomy.

Conclusion:

The relationship between AI and humanity is rife with complexities and challenges. While AI brings immense potential, we must navigate these challenges to ensure its benefits are harnessed to augment human capabilities rather than overshadow or eliminate them. The threats to employment, the implications of humanoid robots on society, ethical dilemmas, loss of human creativity, and dependency on AI are all critical facets that demand careful consideration and proactive measures. To strike a harmonious balance, collaboration between technology developers, policymakers, and society at large is crucial in shaping a future where AI supports and enhances humanity rather than competing against it.

Chapter 6: The Future of AI and the World

Introduction:

As Artificial Intelligence (AI) continues to advance rapidly, its potential implications and impacts on the world are both awe-inspiring and thought-provoking. In this chapter, we will explore the future of AI and its potential applications in various fields, from healthcare to climate change. Through real-world examples, we will delve into the possibilities and challenges that lie ahead, while contemplating the importance of ethical considerations, responsible development, and the role of AI in shaping a sustainable future.

1. Healthcare Revolution:

AI is poised to revolutionize healthcare by transforming diagnosis, treatment, and patient care. For instance, AI algorithms can analyze medical data, identify patterns, and assist in accurate diagnoses. In oncology, AI systems can analyze vast amounts of genomic data to provide personalized treatment plans. Additionally, AI-powered robotic devices can enhance surgical precision and reduce complications. The utilization of AI in healthcare has the potential to improve patient outcomes, enhance access to healthcare in underserved areas, and increase the overall efficiency of the healthcare system.

2. Environmental Preservation and Climate Change:

AI can play a crucial role in addressing environmental challenges and combating climate change. For example, AI-powered systems can analyze satellite imagery to monitor deforestation, track endangered species, and identify areas at risk of disasters. AI algorithms can also optimize energy consumption, leading to more efficient utilization of resources. Furthermore, AI can assist in the development of renewable energy technologies and contribute to sustainable urban planning by optimizing transportation routes and reducing carbon emissions.

3. Enhanced Education:

AI has the potential to transform education by personalizing learning experiences and enabling adaptive teaching methods. Intelligent tutoring systems can analyze student performance data and provide tailored feedback and guidance. Education chatbots can answer students' questions and provide additional resources, supplementing traditional classroom instruction. AI can also facilitate the development of virtual reality (VR) and augmented reality (AR) tools, revolutionizing immersive learning experiences. By harnessing AI in education, we can enhance accessibility, cater to individual learning needs, and foster lifelong learning.

4. Efficient Transportation and Mobility:

Advancements in AI and autonomous systems hold the promise of revolutionizing transportation and mobility. Self-driving cars and smart traffic management systems can optimize traffic flow, reduce congestion, and enhance road safety. Moreover, AI algorithms can predict travel patterns and optimize public transportation schedules, minimizing waiting times and improving overall efficiency. Shared mobility services, enabled by AI algorithms, can further reduce traffic congestion and carbon emissions, contributing to sustainable and efficient transportation systems.

5. Social and Economic Equality:

AI has the potential to address societal inequalities by improving access to resources and opportunities. For instance, AI-powered language translation tools can break language barriers, enabling communication and collaboration across cultures. AI algorithms can help bridge the digital divide by providing access to information and services in underserved areas. Moreover, AI can assist in identifying and mitigating biases in decision-making processes, leading to fairer outcomes in areas such as hiring and loan approvals, minimizing social inequalities.

Conclusion:

The future of AI holds immense possibilities for transforming various aspects of our lives. From revolutionizing healthcare and addressing environmental challenges to enhancing education and improving transportation systems, AI has the potential to bring about significant positive change.

However, as we embrace these possibilities, it is crucial to prioritize ethical considerations, responsible development, and the human-centric approach to ensure AI serves the best interests of humanity. By fostering collaboration between technologists, policy-makers, and society, we can shape a future where AI is harnessed responsibly, contributing to a more sustainable, equitable, and prosperous world.

Conclusion

In conclusion, AI Billionaire: The New Normal showcases how artificial intelligence is transforming and disrupting various industries, leading to the emergence of new billionaires in the technology sector. This documentary sheds light on how AI is changing the game for businesses and individuals alike, and how the world is adapting to this rapidly evolving technology. As we move forward, it is crucial to maintain a balance between the benefits of AI and the potential risks that come with it. We must ensure that AI is used ethically and responsibly to create a brighter and more sustainable future. With its promising potential, artificial intelligence is definitely the new normal, and we must embrace the opportunities it offers to shape our world for the better.